IMAGES
of America

PORTSMOUTH

SOUSA
AND
HIS BAND

John Philip Sousa 1892 JOHN PHILIP SOUSA John Philip Sousa 1920

Lieut.-Commander, U. S. N. R. F.

"Sousa is an Institution. His Band is an Inspiration.
He Ranks Among the First Composers of the Day."—N. Y. Sun.

1892 | 28th SEASON | 1920

FAMOUS THE WORLD AROUND

The Paris Exposition
The Columbian World's Fair
The St. Louis Exposition
The Glasgow Exposition
The Buffalo Pan-American Exposition
The Atlanta Cotton Exposition
The Panama-Pacific Exposition
One Entire Year New York Hippodrome
Four European Tours, 1900-01-03-05
One World's Tour Encircling the Globe, 1911-12

Colonial Theatre, PORTSMOUTH **Matinee Only** **THURSDAY ...AUGUST 12**

IMAGES
of America

PORTSMOUTH

Compiled by
Gerald D. Foss

ARCADIA

First published 1994
Reprinted 1998
Copyright © Gerald D. Foss, 1994

ISBN 07524 0061 4

Published by Arcadia Publishing,
an imprint of the Chalford Publishing Corporation,
One Washington Center, Dover, New Hampshire 03820.
Printed in Great Britain

Other publications by Gerald D. Foss
Three Centuries of Freemasonry in New Hampshire (1972)
Colonial Freemasonry (1977) (Co-author)
and many magazine articles on the history of New Hampshire.

Dedicated to
JAMES EDMUND WHALLEY
Benefactor of the James E. Whalley Museum and Library
My friend, mentor, and Masonic sponsor

Contents

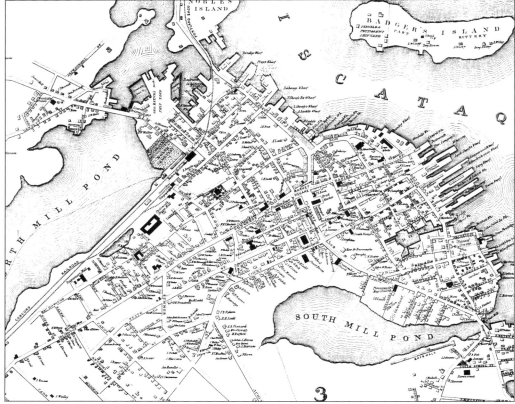

This map of the centre of Portsmouth was excerpted from that published by Charles W. Brewster in 1850, from the original surveys directed by Civil Engineer H.F. Walling.

Acknowledgments

The photographs of Portsmouth shown in this book represent a small portion of a collection owned by or on loan to the James E. Whalley Museum and Library. Credit is given to the United States Navy and the United States Coast Guard for photographs taken by these services for which permission has been given to reproduce. Similarly, our thanks to the New Hampshire Historical Society for photographs obtained from them.

By a special vote of St. John's Lodge No. 1 passed on May 4, 1994, those photographs owned by it and on loan to James E. Whalley Museum and Library are reproduced with permission. A special thanks is expressed to other Masonic bodies in the Portsmouth area, including St. Andrew's Lodge No. 56, for photographs reproduced within.

The lack of space does not permit us to acknowledge the many donors who have given old photographs of Portsmouth over the past twenty-five years. These gifts by various individuals have made this repository a valuable part of the heritage of this Seacoast city.

Trustees, James E. Whalley Museum and Library.

Introduction

I have included here a brief history of Portsmouth, which I hope will enhance your understanding and pleasure in viewing this selection of photographs.

In 1623 the first settlers arrived and established their homes at what is now Odiorne' Point, at the entrance to Portsmouth Harbor. Others would follow and use the present island of New Castle as a place to live. The original settlement in Portsmouth was called Strawbery Banke because of the abundance of wild strawberries on the bank of the Piscataqua River. Slowly but surely the population increased and by 1653 there was a sufficient number of residents to petition the General Court of Massachusetts to call the above settlements Portsmouth, and the petition was granted.

The Piscataqua River and adjacent waters were teeming with fish and crustaceans: white fish, cod, clams, crabs, lobsters and others were plentiful for the labor. Rich soil provided excellent vegetable harvests and wild berries were abundant in season. Thick forests provided wood for fuel, homes, boats and seagoing vessels. For quite some time business revolved around fishing, logging, producing lumber and the making of potash.

Each family needed a small boat for fishing and the demand for small merchant vessels to carry on trade caused the boat and shipbuilding industry to flourish. When England wanted a naval vessel the HMS *Falkland* was built on North Mill Pond.

By 1750 trade prospered and merchant ships transported cargoes to the Caribbean Islands. Other cargo ships plied the seas to England and Europe. After discharging their cargoes the captains would fill their ships with merchandise needed in the settlement of New Hampshire and return to Portsmouth Harbor. Some interprovincial trading also transpired with the ports of New York, Philadelphia, Savannah and Charleston.

On numerous occasions the citizens of Portsmouth were required to defend themselves and their settlement against hostile Indian attacks. They also fought valiantly for King George II during the French and Indian Wars. In 1765, when England imposed a tax on tea, trouble was brewing. The so-called Stamp Act was read in Portsmouth's Haymarket Square.

The successful attack on the small British garrison in Fort William and Mary on New Castle Island on December 13 and 14, 1774, was the overt act which marked the beginning of the American Revolution. The leaders of the attack were John Langdon and John Sullivan, both of whom served in the Continental Congress and as governors of New Hampshire. The muskets, gunpowder and cannon which were captured were later used in the Battle of Bunker Hill.

During the Revolution shipbuilding continued to be a major industry in Portsmouth. Three vessels were built for the Continental Navy: the frigate *Raleigh,* the sloop-of-war *Ranger* and the seventy-four-gun ship *America.* At this time the town was thriving. Portsmouth ranked twelfth in population when the first census was taken by the United States Government in 1790, and its prosperity and growth was dependent for many years on sea trade.

Following the War of 1812, a decided change in occupations occurred when local men turned to the manufacture of many items heretofore imported, such as furniture, silverware, stoves and other necessities. Samuel Dockum was a well-known maker of furniture in this era; others built clipper ships to speed transportation to foreign ports. The Portsmouth Naval Shipyard continued at a slow pace to build ships for the United States Navy. The outbreak of the war between the states saw an incredible increase in employment at the Shipyard. The first naval ship built here to use steam as well as sails was the USS *Kearsarge.*

After the war was over, several new manufacturing plants were erected in the city, including breweries, shoe shops, and the Morley Button Company, the largest manufacturer of buttons in the world. The introduction of gas and electricity as well as the telephone brought about changes in lifestyles. Likewise, the invention and spread of the train and the automobile meant significant changes in industry and occupations. Before the outbreak of war in Europe in 1914, the Shipyard had been authorized to build a new type of naval fighting vessel known as the submarine. There would be an ever increasing number of such boats until 1969 when the last nuclear-powered submarine, *Sand Lance*, was launched.

The photographs in this book have been classified to give a logical arrangement and also a feel for the history of Portsmouth through the more than 350 years since the first settlers arrived. The selection has been made from a collection administered by the James E. Whalley Museum and Library, which is open to the public and is located in the Masonic Temple, 351 Middle Street, in Portsmouth. The James E. Whalley Museum and Library was established by a provision in the will of James E. Whalley, 'that a non-profit corporation be formed to establish a library and museum with emphasis on books and artifacts of a historic and Masonic nature.'

Gerald D. Foss

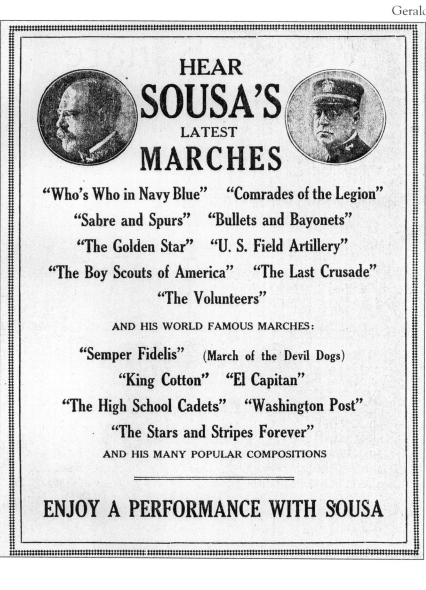

One
Market Square

The Old State House was erected in 1758 when Market Square was known as King Street. In 1789 President George Washington addressed the citizens of Portsmouth from the balcony over the door on the end of the building.

Market Square looking south on Pleasant Street showing the drinking fountain for horses. Market Square has been a focal point in Portsmouth for three centuries and continues to play an important role as a downtown center of activity.

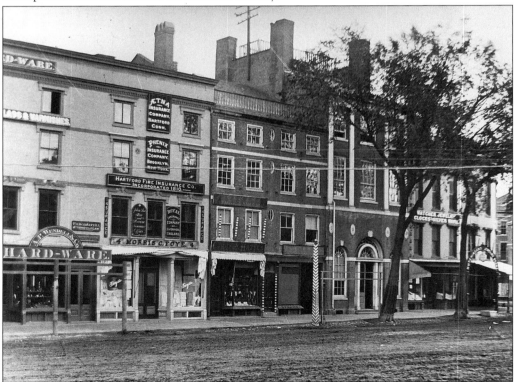

Market Square, c. 1880. The Foye store existed for three generations.

Market Square looking towards the northeast along Market Street around 1920.

Another view of Market Square looking towards the northeast along Market Street around 1920. All trolley cars used Market Square as a terminal between 1895 and 1925.

The New Hampshire Bank building was erected in 1803. This photograph must have been taken around 1900: on the right can be seen a portion of the old City Hall which was removed in 1912.

Market Square at Christmas time in 1948. After being dark during the war years, by this time lights have returned. However, note the sign on the roof showing the need for men in the US Army and Air Force.

Market Square looking down Market Street in October 1920. Notice the sign on the drinking fountain: 'PORTSMOUTH WELCOMES YOU. WHY LEAVE?' An early bus appears at the right in front of Grace's Drug Store.

13

The Peduzzi Building at the corner of High Street and Congress Street was demolished in 1890.

This four-story building was erected around 1900 to replace the Peduzzi Building at 1 Congress Street. The first floor was occupied by John H. Taylor, Confectioner, and the second floor by a dentist. Known as Fay's Block, it was later occupied by the National Mechanics and Traders Bank which was then bought by the First National Bank in 1931.

Market Square, *c.* 1921. By this time, parking motor vehicles was already starting to become a problem.

Market Square looking south on Pleasant Street in the early 1920s. A mixture of motor vehicles and horse-drawn carriages can be seen in this photograph.

Market Street looking up High Street around 1880. Many well-known businesses are advertised here.

Market Square looking west on Congress Street.

Market Square after the severe ice storm of 1886. Fallen branches and a one-horse sleigh can be seen in this winter scene.

Market Square after the severe ice storm of January 28 and 29, 1886.

Market Square looking down Congress Street in 1886.

Market Square in transition: looking down Congress Street, *c.* 1925. Three modes of transportation indicate the gradual change from the use of horses, to trolley cars, to automobiles.

North Church was erected in 1854. This photograph shows a man painting the weathervane on the top of the steeple.

MARKET SQ AND CONGRES ST.

OCT. 15 192

Market Square decorated with flags and bunting in observance of the Bektash Temple Shrine ceremonial session on October 15, 1920.

Two
Street Scenes

An aerial view of Portsmouth taken in 1970 showing the Piscataqua River with Badger's Island in the middle. In the upper portion of the picture is a part of Portsmouth Naval Shipyard. From the early years of settlement, Market Square has been the center of the city and as we see here, it still is. US Route 1 runs through the center of Portsmouth on its long journey from Maine to Florida.

Market Street looking south to Bow Street in 1877. This scene is about opposite the Moffatt-Ladd House. Although distillers still exist, one would find it difficult to find a sail loft such as that seen next to Wm. Ward & Sons.

Market Street, *c.* 1888. This commercial district was a popular place to purchase crockery, stationery, clothing and groceries for many years. Its focus has changed with the domination of malls and out-of-town plazas to include more tourist-orientated stores, but it retains a bustling atmosphere.

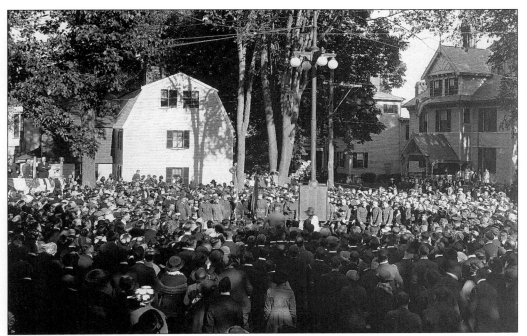

The World War I memorial tablet was dedicated in Haymarket Square on September 19, 1920 to the citizens of Portsmouth who served in the armed forces during World War I. It has since been relocated to Goodwin Park.

Haymarket Square, c. 1923. One building remains today, namely the John Paul Jones House (Portsmouth Historical Society) in the center-left background. The brick wall on the left side of the photograph is the Middle Street Baptist Church. The church has since been demolished.

North Mill on Maplewood Avenue. The mill, operated by fresh water coming from Bartlett Street through North Mill Pond, was used for grinding grain and for woodworking in the mid-1800s.

North Mill on Maplewood Avenue.

North Mill Pond, where many small ships were built between 1749 and 1855. The large house with four chimneys was called the Boyd-Raynes House. It was built by Colonel Nathaniel Meserve around 1740. His shipyard was in the rear of his house and here in 1749 he built the fifty-gun Man-of-War *America* for the Royal Navy. In 1832 George Raynes bought the shipyard and built between sixty and seventy vessels. The large white building in the center of the photograph is the Old Grist Mill.

A section of Atlantic Heights was built in 1918 to accommodate workmen (and their families) who were engaged in building warships for the US Navy on the Piscataqua River. Most of these houses were built largely of brick. When World War I ended in 1918 the US Government sold them by auction. The barracks in the foreground were for the workmen who built the brick houses.

'Newspaper Row' on State Street, *c.* 1868. Joshua Foster was editor of *The States and Union* when he decided to publish an afternoon paper which he called *The Daily Times*. One of his descendants, Robert Foster, now publishes a daily known as *Foster's Daily Democrat* in Dover.

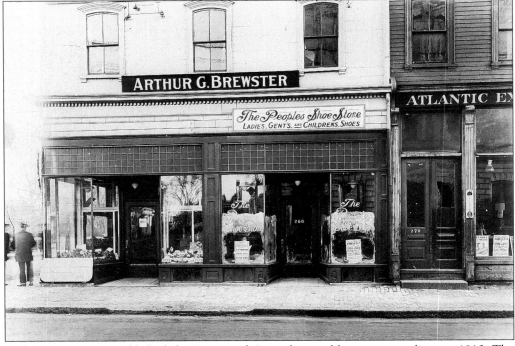

Arthur G. Brewster published the *Portsmouth Journal*, a weekly newspaper, here in 1910. The location is the corner of State and Pleasant Streets.

Circus elephants walk south on Pleasant Street, *c.* 1905. North Church is in the background.

The circus came to Portsmouth, *c.* 1905. This is Market Square looking north with Moorcroft's Millinery Store in the background.

Market Street looking towards Bow Street, *c.* 1888. Notice stores such as George B. French, John S. Rand and Lewis E. Staples, all in business at that time.

Old Spring Market on Ceres Street as it appeared *c.* 1870. Later the market became a ferry landing for the Portsmouth, Kittery and York Street Railway.

William R. Preston and his son Andrew P. Preston operated an apothecary shop in Congress Block for several years. This picture was taken about 1880.

President William Howard Taft visiting Portsmouth on October 23, 1912. Guarded by local policemen, he gave an address to a crowd of adults and children on Parrott Avenue after returning from a visit to Portsmouth Naval Ship yard where he received a twenty-one-gun salute.

President William Howard Taft being received by a large crowd in front of the Rockingham Hotel on October 23, 1912. The mayor of Portsmouth, the Hon. Daniel W. Badger, invited him for lunch that day.

A parade of the Knights Templar on Congress Street, *c.* 1926. The buildings nearest to North Church, with the sole exception of Eagle Studio, are gone. Some burned; others, like the Colonial Theater, were demolished.

An aerial view of Portsmouth. This is the south end of the city showing the Piscataqua River and South Mill Pond on the left and North Mill Pond in the upper left corner. Two of the three bridges crossing the river into Maine can be seen.

A 1910 scene showing the old and new modes of transportation. The decorations were put up to welcome the return of the Sons and Daughters of Portsmouth, who for one reason or another had become residents of other towns and cities. The site is called South Mill Pond Bridge, an old part of the city. Many of the buildings were erected prior to the American Revolution.

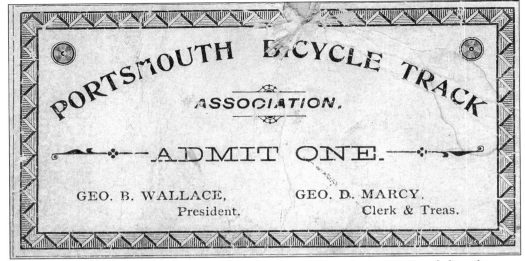

A Portsmouth Bicycle Track Association ticket to admit one person to watch bicycle races, *c.* 1908.

The Portsmouth Bicycle Track was located off Newcastle Avenue. This photograph dates from *c.* 1908.

Called the first 'bus line' in New Castle, this operation was owned by Major David Urch. The power was furnished by a Studebaker auto trailing a jitney made up of a Ford Model T frame with wicker seats.

New Castle's first bus service, *c.* 1912. A Studebaker touring car pulls two jitneys, perhaps to Portsmouth or on a tour of New Castle. The waiting room behind the second jitney is called the 'Wait-A-While.'

A fire scene showing a horse-drawn fire engine pumping water on Downing's Sea Grill and Chop House at 111 Congress Street, *c.* 1910. Dondero's Fruit Store and Hassett's Music Store appear to have sustained damage.

Maplewood Garage on Vaughan Street after a fire, *c.* 1926.

Three
Taverns and Hotels

Stoodley's Tavern was erected in 1761 to replace a similar building which was destroyed by fire. It is famous as the meeting place of the Sons of Liberty who gathered here to prepare for the attack on Fort William and Mary in Portsmouth Harbor on December 14, 1774. The building was moved to Strawbery Banke in 1964 and is being restored.

The Earl of Halifax Tavern was erected by John Stavers in 1767/8. He rented the third floor to St. John's Lodge, F. & A.M. until the Revolutionary War began. He was a loyalist but did not leave the country. Only after a disturbance allegedly caused by the Sons of Liberty did he flee briefly to a nearby town but he soon returned to the tavern and to the housing of men who arrived here to help the Colonies wage war against England. This photograph was taken around 1895.

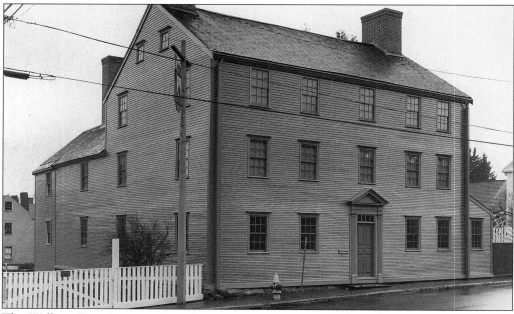

The William Pitt Tavern, originally known as the Earl of Halifax Tavern. This tavern was restored in 1987 by donations made by Freemasons of New Hampshire. The building is now owned by Strawbery Banke Museum, but the upper two stories are leased to the Grand Lodge of New Hampshire, F. & A.M. for fifty years.

The Langdon House on the corner of Congress and Vaughan Streets. It was replaced by the Worth building.

The Kearsarge House was erected in 1866 on Congress Street. Construction of the hotel was supervised by the well-known local builder of the nineteenth century, Benjamin F. Webster.

This view shows the front and west side of the Kearsarge House.

This view of the Kearsarge House shows the front and east side of the old hotel. The east side is on Chestnut Street. The building next to it is the Music Hall, which is now used as a cinema and theater. A portion of the building on the corner of Congress and Chestnut Streets was an express company operated by Carll & Co. It was replaced by the Hartford Block around 1924.

The Globe Tavern at Portsmouth Plains. This old building had several names as a tavern from as early as 1760. Note the utility pole which carries an arm for the trolley cars which passed the Plains prior to 1926.

The prestigious Rockingham Hotel was erected in 1886 by local brewer Frank Jones to replace a hotel which had been on the site since 1830. The two busts in the peaks are those of Woodbury Langdon and Frank Jones. The hotel is decorated for the Kearsarge-Alabama celebration on September 18, 1900. It has now been converted to condominiums.

Four
Historic Buildings

The John Paul Jones House, so-called because Captain John Paul Jones boarded here, with the Purcell family, while awaiting completion of the naval ship *Ranger* in 1777. After some engagements in European waters, Jones was commissioned to take command of the ship *America*, a seventy-four-gun ship of the line. He returned to Portsmouth once again to stay with Mrs. Gregory Purcell and her family.

The John Langdon House was erected in 1774 by John Langdon, a shipbuilder and one of Portsmouth's most famous residents. Langdon was a strong leader of the American Revolution. He served in the Continental Congress, was governor of New Hampshire from 1788 to 1801, and was a signer of the US Constitution.

The Captain Hopley Yeaton residence, believed to have been erected on Deer Street in 1725. Yeaton purchased it in 1769 for his wife and family from the estate of Susanna Pitman. Upon his re-assignment to Lubec, Maine in 1798, he sold it to Captain Nathaniel Kennard. It has since been moved across Deer Street to be used as a Senior Citizens Center, and is now known as the Sherburne House.

Fire buckets of the Federal Fire Society. The society was founded in 1789 and is still in existence. These buckets were not only the water containers used by the 'Bucket Brigade' but when empty they were used to store mops made of woolen cloth and turn-screws for taking down bedsteads.

The Portsmouth Athenaeum in Market Square. The three-story building was erected in 1804 to house the New Hampshire Insurance Company. It was sold about 1823 to the Portsmouth Athenaeum to be used as a library. Today it is supported by shareholders who pay annual dues and by the income from various funds.

The reading room in the Portsmouth Athenaeum. In this room prominent men came to read newspapers and books and to learn the news of the town and nation as related by travelers.

A different view of the reading room. It is still used as a quiet place for study by the members of the Athenaeum.

The Frank Jones Brewery on Islington Street. The inset is a likeness of owner Frank Jones (1832–1902). Jones owned the Rockingham Hotel and the Wentworth Hotel, and as mayor of Portsmouth in 1868/69 and a member of Congress from 1875 to 1879, he became one of the most prominent citizens of Portsmouth.

The Frank Jones Brewery rope-pulling team. The heavy line and belt used in this sport require the physical qualities evidenced by its members.

Eldredge's Brewery on Cate Street as it appeared *c.* 1900. It was second in production to the Frank Jones Brewery. This building now houses a law firm, an engineering firm and an insurance business.

The Portsmouth Brewing Company on Bow Street as it appeared *c.* 1880. It was the smallest of the city's three major breweries. There has recently been a revival of interest in local and independent brewing in Portsmouth and beyond.

An interior view of the *Portsmouth Daily Times*, c. 1900. Here type was set into sections for the newspaper before they had linotype machines.

Another interior view of the *Portsmouth Daily Times*, c. 1900. This newspaper was printed from 1868 until 1925, when it was purchased by the *Portsmouth Herald*.

The Samuel Larkin House. Samuel Larkin became wealthy as an auctioneer of cargoes taken from Portsmouth privateers during the War of 1812. This house was built *c.* 1815.

The residence of Wallace Hackett (1856–1939), a lawyer and also a mayor of Portsmouth from 1907 to 1908. The house was built in 1892 by Wilberforce Ireland, a contractor from Manchester, New Hampshire. The property was purchased by St. John's Lodge No. 1, F. & A.M., in 1920.

Franklin Block on Congress Street. Erected in 1820, it was destroyed by fire in 1879. A portion of it was operated as a terminal for stagecoaches from Boston, Portland and Concord.

The Franklin Block was rebuilt on the same site as the previous building. It is occupied by various retail stores on the first floor and offices on the second and third floors. At one time in the 1920s a dance floor on the second story was used for basketball games. The block also housed a movie theater in the mid-1900s.

The Governor Benning Wentworth Mansion. This mansion, located on Little Harbor Road, was erected in 1750 by Governor Benning Wentworth while he was serving as governor of the Province of New Hampshire from 1741 to 1767. It is now owned by the State of New Hampshire.

Governor Wentworth used this room in the mansion as his office.

John H. Bartlett (1869–1952) was governor of New Hampshire from 1919 to 1921. He resided in Portsmouth for many years.

The residence of John H. Bartlett on Middle Street in Portsmouth. Bartlett was born on March 15, 1869 in Sunapee, New Hampshire and died in Portsmouth in 1952. He held several federal positions in Washington, D.C., and was president of an insurance company and a savings bank. Unfortunately this building was demolished about 1958.

Portsmouth Machine Company, c. 1888. The company was located on Hill Street opposite Pearl Street.

Portsmouth Shoe Company was off Islington Street opposite Columbia Street. An important industry to the city, its capacity at peak was 175 60-pair cases of shoes per day. The building was demolished c. 1937.

The old US post office and customs building was erected in 1858. Its cornerstone was laid by the Grand Lodge of New Hampshire, F. & A.M. The architect was the famous Ammi B. Young whose work may be seen in many US cities. The building was sold to a private owner *c.* 1972 and the post office is now located on Daniel Street.

Rockingham County Court House was erected on State Street in 1891. It housed the superior court and the probate court for Rockingham County. Governor John McLane tendered a reception in this building in 1905 to the delegates from Russia and Japan who were here to negotiate the Treaty of Portsmouth. The building was demolished in 1968.

The Moffatt-Ladd House on Market Street. It was occupied by William Whipple until his death in 1785. Whipple was a signer of the Declaration of Independence. The small building to the right was a counting house.

A chestnut tree in the backyard of the Moffatt-Ladd House on Market Street. There is also a beautiful flower garden here that blooms each summer.

57

The original Congress Block was built by Samuel Coues in 1859 and housed various busy stores and businesses. The top floor was leased to St. John's Lodge No. 1 and St. Andrew's Lodge No. 56 for twenty-five years. When it was destroyed by fire in 1865, Coues decided not to rebuild it. Another Congress Block was erected on the site by a syndicate of prominent men of Portsmouth.

The Neal Block replaced a much older building at the intersection of State and Fleet Streets c. 1920. It was erected by Cecil M. Neal, one-time mayor of Portsmouth, who operated the auto supply store. The drug store was owned by William D. Grace. The site is now a parking lot for Portsmouth Savings Bank. Although many of Portsmouth's historic buildings have been preserved, a huge number have been lost due to the demands of traffic and development.

The Hart House was erected around 1740 and was badly damaged by fire in 1761. It was better known as 'Noah's Ark' as it was occupied by Noah Parker during the American Revolution. It was located at the corner of Ark, now Penhallow, Street and Daniel Street.

The Treadwell House was erected in 1758 on the corner of State and Fleet Streets by Mrs. Charles Treadwell for her son Nathaniel. Later it was occupied by the Davenport Inn. In the twentieth century the YWCA used it. It was moved to Court Street for the law firm of Waldron, Boynton & Waldron c. 1957.

The Jaffrey House on Linden Street was erected *c.* 1730 by George Jaffrey, II who was born in New Castle. Jaffrey was treasurer of the Province of New Hampshire and a chief justice of the superior court. The house was demolished *c.* 1967 to allow construction of the Federal Building. Linden Street intersected with Daniel Street near the former City Hall.

The Jonathan Warner House was erected in 1716 by Archibald MacPheadris, a member of the King's Council in 1722. MacPheadris' daughter Mary, a widow, married Jonathan Warner, a widower, in 1760. Warner was also a member of the King's Council until the Revolution. This stately Georgian mansion is considered to be one of the finest remaining eighteenth-century urban brick residences.

The Boston and Maine Railroad station, c. 1900. Eight passenger trains passed through here each weekday at the peak of its operation. Some trains traveled between Boston and Halifax, Nova Scotia via Portsmouth. All stopped here to take on water as well as to take on and leave passengers.

The Boston and Maine Railroad steam locomotive No. 385 with baggage car and passenger car attached, in Portsmouth rail yard c. 1905.

The Tobias Lear House on Hunking Street. Lear (1760–1816) was George Washington's private secretary between 1785 and 1799.

The Samuel Cushman House was erected in 1790 on the west side of Washington Street. Cushman (1783–1851) served as a congressman between 1835 and 1839.

Five

The Piscataqua River and Portsmouth Harbor

Fort Point Lighthouse. This is located at the entrance to Portsmouth Harbor. There has been a lighthouse here since 1771 although several changes have been made over the years.

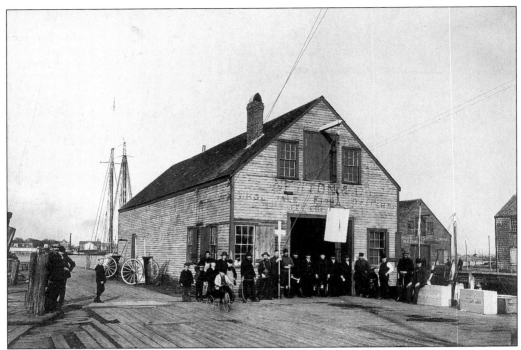

Workers gathered outside the buildings of Newton & Co. Wholesale Fish Dealers, *c.* 1888. This was located on Commercial Wharf off Marcy Street next to Prescott Park. A portion of Portsmouth Naval Shipyard can be seen across the river.

Portsmouth waterfront, *c.* 1897. Note the Franklin Shiphouse at Portsmouth Naval Shipyard in the background.

A Portsmouth waterfront scene off the south end of town, *c.* 1920. Newcastle Avenue is in the center of the photograph with the bridge to New Castle at the top left.

An ice jam in the Piscataqua River during the winter of 1918 damaged the aquarium located beside New Castle Bridge. This toll bridge was operated by Major David Urch for many years.

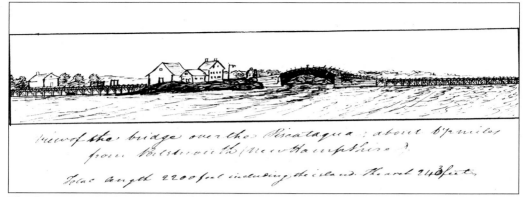

View of the bridge over the Piscataqua; about 6½ miles from Portsmouth (New Hampshire). Total length 2200 feet including the island. The arch 243 feet.

The Piscataqua Bridge in 1794. This is a sketch of the first bridge built to cross the Piscataqua River. It spanned from Fox Point in Newington to Goat Island. A continuation of the bridge terminated in Durham, at which point there is an historical marker. A draw span was on the Durham end of the bridge to permit the passage of larger ships. Swept away from Great Bay by ice in 1855, it was never rebuilt. (Sketch by Robert Gilmore.)

The ferry *Mineola* sailing up the Piscataqua River to Portsmouth. The naval prison may be seen to the right of a water tower at the Shipyard.

The Russian-Japanese peace conference building located at Portsmouth Naval Shipyard. Here the Treaty of Portsmouth was negotiated and signed in 1905.

Russian and Japanese ambassadors who came to Portsmouth at the invitation of President Theodore Roosevelt to secure the peace treaty which ended the Russian-Japanese War. They succeeded. Here they are seated around the table in the peace conference building at Portsmouth Naval Shipyard.

Building quay walls at the Shipyard, c. 1900–10. The horse and wagon suspended in midair were used to transport rock fill.

The ruins of the Franklin Shiphouse at the Shipyard as it appeared in 1936. This building was a landmark visible from Portsmouth and Kittery for many years. The central part of Kittery may be seen across the river. (Official photograph, US Navy)

Laying the first granite block in the building of Dry Dock No. 2 at the Shipyard, *c.* 1900. (Official photograph, US Navy)

Six
Governmental

Abner Greenleaf (1785–1868), president of the New Hampshire State Senate. Greenleaf, a newspaper editor by trade, became the first mayor of Portsmouth in 1850.

Portsmouth High School was erected in 1858 at the corner of Chapel and Daniel Streets. It was subsequently used as City Hall from 1907 to 1991 and is now privately owned.

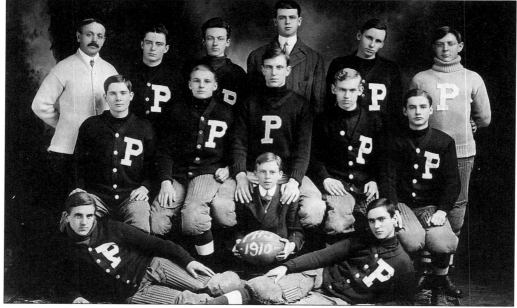

Portsmouth High School basketball team in 1910.

The second high school was erected in 1907 on Islington Street. The building is now an apartment complex for senior citizens known as Farragut Apartments.

Farragut School at the intersection of High Street and School Street was named in honor of Admiral David Farragut. Erected in 1889 as a grade school, it was demolished in the 1970s as part of an 'Urban Renewal' development.

The Haven School was built *c.* 1846 on South Street for children in the elementary grades.

The Franklin School was erected in 1847 on Maplewood Avenue, and was a grade school for children in that area. Note the tower on the schoolhouse. The New Franklin School has been built to replace it. Both the Franklin School and the Haven School are now used for residential purposes.

Portsmouth High School class of 1923. Holding the class banner are: (from left to right) John B. Pike, Charlotte Tasker, Dorothy Madison and Herbert E. Richardson.

Portsmouth High School class of 1928. Behind the banner are the class officers: (from left to right) Malcolm McLachlan, Geraldine (Conner) Hartford, Edith (McKenna) Hagstrom and Walker Goodrich.

William Whipple (1730–1785) was a signer of the Declaration of Independence. He served as a brigadier general in several battles during the American Revolution.

The Whipple School was erected in 1887 and was named for William Whipple. In the early years it was used for grades seven and eight only. This entrance to the school is on State Street at the corner of Summer Street. The building is now privately owned as condominiums.

Portsmouth High School band posing in front of the high school on Islington Street in 1936.

Participants in the David Kushious School of Music in front of the Rockingham Hotel on State Street.

Portsmouth Junior High School was erected in 1932 for grades seven, eight and nine. Now known as Portsmouth Middle School, it houses grades six, seven and eight. It is located on Parrott Avenue.

Portsmouth High School was built in 1955 and is still in use today. It is located on Alumni Drive.

This old wood waterpipe was used by Portsmouth Aqueduct Co., a privately owned corporation until it was sold to the City of Portsmouth in 1893.

Wibird Penhallow (1791–1867), author of the first town of Portsmouth directory in 1821. He resided on Water Street at that time.

Ichabod Goodwin (1796–1882) was a sea captain for fifteen years as a young man. Once settled ashore he entered mercantile business at which he was very successful, becoming president of several large corporations including the First National Bank and the Piscataqua Savings Bank. In politics he served in the state legislature for six terms and became governor of New Hampshire in 1859.

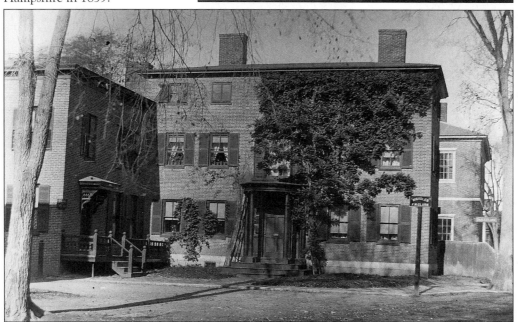

The Benedict House. It was built on Middle Street prior to 1839 and occupied by Robert LeFavour, who was the city treasurer for many years. It is named for Dr. Frank E. Benedict, MD, who occupied the house in the early 1900s. It is now a part of Portsmouth Public Library.

Portsmouth Chemical Fire Wagon No. 5 was always ready to have horses hitched to it to rush to a fire. It is believed to have been one of the last horse-drawn fire wagons in Portsmouth prior to the use of motorized fire trucks.

Willard J. Sampson Hook and Ladder Company No. 1, *c*. 1916. This photograph was taken on Parrott Avenue. The hose tower of the firehouse can be seen in the background.

The McIntosh Block on fire during the afternoon of May 5, 1931. When the fire was extinguished nothing but a portion of the brick walls remained. Sparks from this tremendous fire set off thirty-five other fires in the north end of Portsmouth. The block was rebuilt by Duncan H. McIntosh after the fire.

The Exchange Block on fire in 1941. Located on Pleasant Street opposite the post office building, it attracted quite a crowd on a Sunday noon.

Seven

Older Houses of Worship

St. John's Church (Episcopal) was erected in 1807 to replace Queen's Chapel, which was erected in 1732 and was destroyed by fire on Christmas Eve, 1806.

An interior view of St. John's Church. There are many ancient artifacts here which are actually older than the church building, such as the baptismal font, the 'Vinegar' Bible and the mahogany chair within the chancel.

The Brattle Organ in St. John's Church. It was built in England in 1662 and was imported by Thomas Brattle for use in his home sometime before 1708. St. John's Church acquired it in 1836. It was restored in 1964 and is believed to be the oldest organ in the United States.

The Universalist Church was erected on Pleasant Street in 1808 and destroyed by fire in 1896. Several prominent ministers occupied the pulpit, including the Reverend Hosea Ballou, the founder of the Universalist Church.

A second Universalist Church was erected in 1896. Situated on Pleasant Street, it too was destroyed by fire in 1947. The Reverend Charles Hoyt Dickens was minister in 1896. Later he became an Episcopal Priest, served as a captain in the US Navy (Chaplains Corps) and celebrated his 100th birthday on July 24, 1965.

The new North Meeting House, called the three-decker, was built in 1711–14. In 1745 'the town clock was set going.' It was remodeled in 1837 but torn down in 1854.

North Church on Market Square was erected in 1855 at a cost of $30,000. A new pipe organ was installed and the structure restored in 1890. The 'town clock' was renewed and illuminated in 1893. In 1990 the structure and steeple were again restored at a cost in excess of $180,000.

The Unitarian Church was built in 1824. It has served thousands of citizens of Portsmouth.

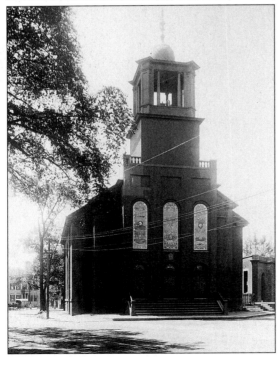

The Middle Street Baptist Church was erected *c.* 1827 and demolished in 1955.

Methodist Church on State Street. The third oldest building in Portsmouth used for religious worship was constructed by Jonathan Barker in 1827 as a Methodist Church. It is now Temple Israel, a Synagogue.

The United Methodist Church was erected *c.* 1912 on Miller Avenue to replace the earlier building on State Street which was sold to members of Temple Israel.

Christ Church (Episcopal) was erected in 1881. Following the signing of the peace treaty of the Russian-Japanese War in 1905, the Russians held peace services here. It was a beautiful building inside as well as outside, but in June 1963 fire reduced it to a pile of stone.

The choirs of St. John's Church and Christ Church pictured in 1933. The choirmaster of St. John's, Ernest P. Bilbruck, is first on the left in the front row. The group is gathered at the entrance to Christ Church on Madison Street.

Eight
The Armed Forces

USS *Constitution* is the oldest commissioned ship in the US Navy. It was built in Boston *c.* 1798 and is now a tourist attraction at Charlestown Naval Shipyard. It was at Portsmouth Naval Shipyard for many years as a receiving ship.

A stern view of USS *Constitution*. This photograph may have been taken when the ship was on a visit to Portsmouth Naval Shipyard following its restoration in 1932.

General Henry Dearborn (1751–1829) studied medicine at Portsmouth with Dr. Hall Jackson. A very competanr man, he served in many battles of the American Revolution, from Bunker Hill to Yorktown. He was secretary of war from 1801 to 1809; senior major general in the US Army during the War of 1812; a minister to Portugal from 1822 to 1824; and a member of Congress from 1793 to 1797.

GEORGE WASHINGTON, President of the United States of America.

TO ALL WHO SHALL SEE THESE PRESENTS, GREETING.

KNOW YE, That reposing special Trust and Confidence in the Integrity, Diligence and good Conduct of *Hopley Yeaton of New Hampshire* ~ ~ ~ ~ ~ I DO APPOINT him *Master* ~ of a Cutter in the Service of the United States, for the Protection of the Revenue; and do authorize and empower him to execute and fulfil the Duties of that Office according to Law; AND TO HAVE AND TO HOLD the said office, with all the Rights and Emoluments thereunto legally appertaining, unto him the said *Hopley Yeaton* ~ ~ during the Pleasure of the President of the United States for the Time being.

IN TESTIMONY whereof I have caused these Letters to be made Patent, and the Seal of the United States to be hereunto affixed. GIVEN under my Hand, at the City of Philadelphia, the *Twenty first* ~ Day of *March* ~ in the Year of our Lord one thousand seven hundred and ninety *one*, and of the Independence of the United States of America the *Fifteenth*.

G Washington

By the President

Th Jefferson

Hopley Yeaton's commission as master of a cutter in the US Revenue Marine Service was issued on March 21, 1791. The cutter to which he was assigned was the *Scammel*. He had served as a sea captain of merchant ships and as a lieutenant in the Continental Navy on the frigate *Raleigh* and the frigate *Deane*. He also served as captain of the US Revenue Marine Service cutters the *Governor Gilman* and the *New Hampshire*.

USS *Kearsarge* was built at Portsmouth Naval Shipyard. The red oak planks used in her construction came from the Mount Kearsarge area in New Hampshire. In 1894 she was ordered to Nicaragua to safeguard US interests in the struggle between Nicaragua and Honduras. The ship ran aground on Roncador Reef 200 miles north of her destination. The vessel was a total loss, but all the crew were saved, including James E. Whalley of Portsmouth.

Spanish prisoners of war interned on Seavey's Island, *c.* 1898.

A collier in dry dock at Portsmouth Naval Shipyard. It was used to carry coal for fuel, heat and power.

USS *Argonaut* was launched at Portsmouth Naval Shipyard in 1928. Here it is being removed from dry dock. (Official photograph, US Navy)

The US Coast Guard station at Portsmouth Harbor with USCG cutters *Active* and *Decisive* secured to the wharf. Rarely are both in harbor at the same time. The site is located adjacent to historic Fort Constitution. (Official photograph, US Coast Guard)

US Coast Guard station at Portsmouth Harbor with cutters *Active* and *Decisive* in port, *c.* 1968. The buildings in the background were used by personnel on shore duty. (Official photograph, US Coast Guard)

US Coast Guard cutter *Active* No. 618 on patrol in 1968. (Official photograph, US Coast Guard)

USS *Scamp* being launched from Portsmouth Naval Shipyard into the Piscataqua River in 1942. (Official photograph, US Navy)

USS *Albacore* 569 was launched in 1953. Its style was radical compared to earlier submarines. It was built to go faster and deeper, yet it was powered by diesel engines. It is now a museum in 'Albacore Park' located off Market Street Extension. (Official photograph, US Navy)

USS *Sculpin* SSN 191 was built at Portsmouth Naval Shipyard in 1938. She was attacked by a Japanese destroyer in December 1943 and severely damaged. Before she sank, about forty of the crew went overboard and became prisoners of war of the Japanese. (Official photograph, US Navy)

USS *Squalus* SS192 being raised from the Atlantic Ocean in 1939. The *Squalus* sank on May 23, 1939 while on sea trials. Of the fifty-nine men aboard, thirty-three survived by being raised in a rescue chamber which was lowered to the sub. She was raised, rebuilt and renamed the USS *Sailfish*, and became renowned for her record during World War II. (Official photograph, US Navy)

USS *Nautilus* SSN 571 made the first submerged crossing of the Artic Ocean under the ice. She departed Pearl Harbor on July 23, 1958, submerged in the Barrow Sea on August 1–and a few days later surfaced northeast of Greenland and went on to Portland, England. She berthed in New York Harbor on August 24, 1958. (Official photograph, US Navy)

USS *Seadragon* SSN 584 was launched from Portsmouth Naval Shipyard in 1958. This submarine made history when she sailed from Portsmouth Harbor on August 1, 1960. She sailed under the ice via the Northwest Passage, the first boat ever to sail under the North Pole from east to west, and reached Nome, Alaska on September 5, 1960. From there she sailed to Pearl Harbor, arriving on September 14, 1960. (Official photograph, US Navy)

Members of the Grand Army of the Republic (GAR) assembled in front of the Masonic Home in 1922. Your attention is called to one of the last local survivors, Joseph Doolittle (fourth from the right). For many years in the early 1900s he was a featured speaker before the students of Portsmouth public schools around Memorial Day.

HMS *Capetown* in 1929. The *Capetown* was said to be the first ship of the Royal Navy to visit Portsmouth Harbor since the American Revolution. There were twenty-two Masons among the crew who were invited to attend a meeting of St. John's Lodge No. 1 on August 15, 1929. They were received warmly by seven hundred local Masons gathered for the occasion. Friendships were made between the crew and their hosts which have lasted for more than a generation. Fernley R.C. Liddicoat, a crew member, made several visits to Portsmouth after World War II and on one visit was made an honorary member of St. John's Lodge No. 1.

Nine

Fraternal

US Armed Forces observance in 1943. Every branch of the armed forces is represented in this photograph. Seated third from the left in the front row is Rear Admiral Thomas Withers, Jr., commandant of Portsmouth Naval Shipyard during much of the World War II period. All of the men pictured here are members of the Masonic fraternity.

The Knights of Columbus Home on Islington Street as it appeared in 1920.

The Elks Home on Pleasant Street in 1920. It is situated on the site of Brewster's Tavern where George Washington slept on his visit to Portsmouth in 1789. The Elks sold this building in 1990.

Thomas Thompson (1739–1809). Born in England, he came to Portsmouth in 1767 and became a sea captain employed by John Langdon. He was commissioned by the Continental Congress as a captain in the Continental Navy and was assigned to the naval ship *Raleigh*. This ship sailed to France for supplies, and after a few engagements with the Royal Navy en route, the *Raleigh* returned to Portsmouth under his command in the spring of 1778.

John Sullivan (1740–1795) was one of the most prominent leaders in the American Revolution. He was a brigadier general and later a major general during the war, and became governor of New Hampshire from 1788 to 1790. He was also elected to be the first Grand Master of the Grand Lodge of Free and Accepted Masons of New Hampshire.

Nathaniel Adams (1756–1829) was the author of *Annals of Portsmouth*, which records important occurrences chronologically from 1621 to 1824.

John Christie (1804–1890) is credited with leading the fraternity of Freemasonry in New Hampshire through the anti-Masonic period of 1826–40. His chief occupation was that of clerk to the commandant of Portsmouth Naval Shipyard. The medals on his jacket are those of Scottish Rite Freemasonry. He was the first New Hampshire Mason to receive the Thirty-third Masonic Degree.

The Masonic Lodge Hall as it appeared in 1894. It was leased from the owners of the Congress Block and used by several different Masonic organizations in Portsmouth.

A wine glass from the William Pitt Tavern. This wine glass was presented to St. John's Lodge *c.* 1910 by Thomas Tredick, who wrote that he was a direct descendant of William Stavers. He also noted that his grandmother, Lucy Appleton Stavers, told that this wine glass was used at the time Governor John Sullivan tendered a reception for President George Washington in 1789.

Masons dressed in costumes of the 1789 period prepare to celebrate the 150th anniversary of the Grand Lodge of New Hampshire which was established in Portsmouth on July 8, 1789. This photograph was taken in front of the Masonic Temple on Middle Street in Portsmouth.

Knight Templars assembled on Congress Street in 1948. This was the occasion of the observance of the 100th anniversary of St. Andrew's Lodge No. 56. The lodge was constituted on June 24, 1848.

The second Congress Block was erected in 1867 and is shown here in 1911. The building was decorated to celebrate the 175th anniversary of the oldest Masonic lodge in New Hampshire.

Laying the cornerstone of the Masonic Temple on Miller Avenue in 1928. This ceremony is rarely performed and is primarily a function of the Grand Lodge of Masons in New Hampshire. The large annex attached to the Hackett residence consisted of an auditorium capable of seating three hundred people on the first floor and a lodge room on the second floor.

James E. Whalley, illustrious potentate of Bektash Temple Shrine of North America being greeted by the Hon. H. Styles Bridges, governor of New Hampshire from 1935 to 1937.

Bektash Temple Shriners and their ladies enjoy a banquet. The Shriners are best known for the operation of a network of hospitals in the United States and Canada where children under eighteen years of age are treated for orthopedic problems and severe burns.

Samuel Dockum (1792–1872) was a
prominent cabinetmaker who was well-
known for the fine furniture he crafted and
for the interior woodwork in the cabins of
the famous clipper ships built in Portsmouth.

Frank Jones (1832–1902) was a very
prominent businessman and politician
whose name is still remembered today.
Among the many businesses he owned
were: the Frank Jones Brewery, the
Rockingham Hotel, the Wentworth Hotel
in New Castle and the Granite State Fire
Insurance Co. Jones was mayor of
Portsmouth from 1868 to 1869 and a
congressman from 1875 to 1879.

Admiral David G. Farragut (1801–1870). Born in Campbell's Station, Tennessee in 1801, he commenced military service in 1810 as a midshipman. He served in the US Navy during the War of 1812 and also in the Civil War. Commissioned a captain in 1855, in 1862 he was given command of the Western Gulf Blockading Squadron which opened the ports of New Orleans, Louisiana and Mobile, Alabama.

FUNERAL NOTICE.

Bro. *Chandler M. Hayford*

St. John's Lodge, No. 1, Portsmouth, N. H.

Will assemble on WEDNESDAY, Aug. 17, A. D. 1870, at 11 o'clock, to attend the Funeral of our deceased Bro., Adm'l D. G. FARRAGUT.
Per order of the Master.

DARK CLOTHES, WHITE GLOVES.
GEO. P. EDNY, Secr'y.

Notice of the funeral of Admiral David G. Farragut. This form was used to notify members of St. John's Lodge to attend a funeral service for a deceased Brother. Admiral Farragut died on August 14, 1870 at Portsmouth Naval Shipyard while on a visit to the commandant. He was one of the great Union naval officers during the Civil War.

This 1923 photograph shows the tercentenary celebration of the founding of Portsmouth. The arch was erected in front of the Masonic Temple on Middle Street by Masons to greet all who attended this great anniversary.

Clyde and Mabel Root, *c.* 1913. These children were left at the age of five and nine years without anyone to care for them. St. John's Lodge placed them in the Chase Home for Children temporarily at the expense of the lodge. The Masons of Portsmouth paid for their entire care until they graduated from Portsmouth High School. Mabel graduated from the high school with honors in the class of 1923.

Masons marching to church in 1936. Since 1755, the Masons of Portsmouth and vicinity have observed the Feast of St. John the Baptist (June 24) almost every year by attending divine service at St. John's Church. This photograph shows a portion of the march as it passes from Middle Street to State Street.

The Portsmouth Chapter, of the Order of Demolay for Boys marching on Congress Street in front of the Franklin Block, c. 1949.

Congress Block, *c*. 1920.

William D. Grace (1860–1950), was pharmacist with a place of business on Market Square for more than forty years. He was president of the New Hampshire Pharmaceutical Association for the years 1903 and 1904.

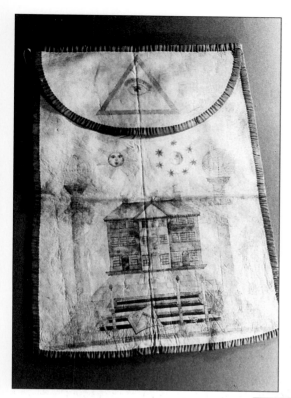

A hand-painted Masonic apron. In addition to many well-known Masonic symbols there is a likeness of a three-story building which might represent a tavern. The identity of the Mason who used this apron is not known.

This apron belonged to Captain James Tarlton of New Castle, who became a Mason in 1812. Most of the symbols on the apron appear to be in gold leaf.

This apron belonged to William Vaughan who became a Mason in 1796. It was handcrafted of silk fabric and decorated with colorful threads.

This apron belonged to Captain Daniel Fernald (1767–1866) who was made a Mason in 1804. He escaped death twice during the War of 1812, once when his ship was boarded by the crew of HMS *Spencer* and again when fired upon by the HMS *Tenedos*.

The Masonic Temple on Miller Avenue was erected in 1928 as an annex to the Masonic Home, formerly the Wallace Hackett residence.

Bicentennial celebration of George Washington's birthday on February 22, 1932. This event was the result of a request by Sol Bloom, congressman from New York, that every state, city and town in the United States do one thing to mark the bicentennial of the birth of George Washington. The Masons of Portsmouth responded by holding a function in which several of the members in colonial costumes represented New Hampshire notables who served under General George Washington. The lodge records report that 725 people attended.

George B. Ward (1905–1973), a Portsmouth native, was a World War II veteran, a successful businessman, a philanthropic citizen, an active churchman and a nationally recognized Masonic leader. Ward was Grand Master of Masons in New Hampshire from 1963 to 1964, and an active member of the Supreme Council of Scottish Rite Freemasonry from 1966 to 1973.

James E. Whalley (1869–1956) was born in Portsmouth and resided here for most of his life. He served in the US Navy and was a longtime US Government employee and city official. Whalley was the leader of several local and state Masonic organizations, and the benefactor of James E. Whalley Museum and Library.